FRANCE

FRANCE
Isabel Bass

Sundial

CONTENTS

First published in 1981 by Octopus Books Ltd
59 Grosvenor Street, London W1

© 1981 Hennerwood Publications Limited

ISBN 0 906320 84 4

Produced by Mandarin Publishers Limited
22a Westlands Road
Quarry Bay. Hong Kong

Printed in Hong Kong

INTRODUCTION

'*Nec Pluribus Impar*' ('I shine on more worlds than one')
Motto of Louis XIV, the Sun King.

France has always consisted of many worlds and many amazing contrasts. Island Britain or boot-shaped Italy are more or less all of a piece, but France's boundaries are not so obvious and the country sprawls across northern and southern Europe.

Its north is sombre and bleak, yet its west is crisp and fresh. And nowhere could be more Mediterranean than Provence with its olive groves, blue skies and the scent of mimosa and lavender in the air.

The people are as diverse as the landscape. The Bretons, descendants of Celtic tribes, are quite different from the easygoing Latin southerners. The Alsatians have much in common with the Germans, the people of the Jura with the Swiss, and the Basques with their Spanish neighbours.

The French heritage, too, is a jumble of many races and tribes. The famous cave paintings in southwest France were produced by prehistoric men and the amphitheatres in the south were constructed by the Romans. Enormous stone crosses in Brittany were put up by the Celts, while Carcassonne has towers built by the Visigoths.

Many more worlds have arisen in just the last 30 years, causing even greater diversity. *La belle France* of happy peasants, fairytale castles and delicious food is now the fifth industrial power in the world. Its skies are punctured with factories alongside graceful cathedral spires. Coastlines are dotted with huge government-planned holiday resorts as well as old fishing villages. *Le supermarché* competes with open air food markets, *le drugstore* and its hamburgers with *la brasserie* and its *prix fixe* menu. As the farms become modernized, the peasant class increasingly dies out. As the country becomes industrialized, once-sleepy provincial towns roar into the 21st century.

Paris, too, contains more worlds than Louis XIV ever dreamed of. A short distance from gothic Notre-Dame cathedral is one of the world's most futuristic buildings, the Centre Beaubourg. Paris skies are silhouetted by skyscrapers as well as by the Sacré-Coeur and the Eiffel Tower, making many worry about 'Manhattan-sur-Seine'.

What forges these contrasting worlds into a single whole? What weaves these pieces into one epic land? What makes modern France as unmistakably French as the olde-worlde peasant one?

Throughout the centuries, France has always adapted outside elements but has transformed them to fit its own ways. It has a clear sense of its own style, a strong national identity, and an aura of continuous civilization. It is a land where each individual acts as if he were king of his own world.

PARIS

'There is never any ending to Paris'
Ernest Hemingway

No city in the world provokes such fascination as
Paris, the capital of France. 'A monster' is how
Parisians refer to this hectic, restless city. From the top
of the Eiffel Tower to the quais of the Seine, it is
crammed with 2,000 years of history, packed with
monuments cherished the world over, and bursting
with people and cars. The noisy press of humanity on the
Boulevard St-Denis (preceding pages), as in all of Paris,
can make daily life an urban nightmare.

Paris owes its existence to the Seine, and its earliest
settlements were on the Ile de la Cité, the island heart
of the city. Twenty centuries later, one of the city's
major problems is to balance its historical legacy with
its modern needs. Lovers of 'old, romantic Paris' fight
against modernistic projects like the architecturally
avant-garde Centre Beaubourg. But town planners
argue that the Eiffel Tower was considered as
outrageous in its day.

Nevertheless, pollution-filled noisy Paris still casts
its magic spell. The appeal is eternally strong, no matter
how much the ideal Paris has been chipped away or
overexposed in songs and films.

Notre-Dame (above) looks like a ship anchored to the
banks of the Seine, a serene edifice that has seen many
great moments. *Te deums* have been sung in this cathedral
for royal marriages and baptisms, candles lit for the
liberation of Paris from the Germans, ceremonies held for
the death of French leaders. Perhaps the most awesome
event that took place in Paris' most beautiful religious
building was Napoleon's coronation as Emperor in 1804.
Breaking with French tradition, he refused to be crowned
at Reims and summoned Pope Pius VII to perform the
ceremony here.

The cathedral is located on the island known as the Ile
de la Cité, and it stands on a site which has been a
religious centre for more than two thousand years. In 1163
the Bishop of Paris, Maurice de Sully, decided to transform
the small church on this spot into a breathtaking
monument. The task took an enormous workforce almost
200 years to complete.

Notre-Dame's most enchanting aspects are its
magnificent stained glass windows, its gargoyles and flying
buttresses, its delicate spire, and its solid sense of calm.
When its 16-ton bell is rung on religious holidays and for
national ceremonies, the austere sound seems to cast a
quiet spell on hyperactive Paris.

Not far down the river is a sight which provoked great
fury when it was erected in 1889. One French playwright,
Jean Giradoux, even called it 'the iron-clad version of the
fakir's rope spiralling up to the heavens'. But the **Eiffel
Tower** (right) is now a much-loved part of the Paris
landscape.

When engineer Gustave Eiffel designed this for the 1889
World Fair, he created the world's tallest structure – 300

metres (984 feet). (Its height was increased to 320 metres in 1957, with the addition of a television antenna.) During its two-year building, sightseers watched with disbelief as workmen joined 12,000 iron girders with 2.5 million rivets to make a 7,000-ton vertical iron spider's nest.

Another kind of craftmanship is what **French fashion** (below) is all about. Designer Yves Saint Laurent has left behind his Moroccan fantasies for more tempered lines, which reveal his brilliant sharp sense of style.

It seems impossible to believe that today's scrambling and shoving in overcrowded salons is not the way things always were in the world of French fashion. But designers used to show collections to formally attired champagne-sipping audiences in a hushed atmosphere.

However, the heyday of *haute-couture* has slipped by, and French designers have recently lost their vice-like grip on the fashion world. In 1970, for example, they introduced the maxi skirt to a world which refused to snap it up. As Italian, American and British designers started to make their mark on the international scene, the French began to adjust to the changing times by opening their own boutiques with ready-to-wear clothes.

This has meant that a Dior suit, a Courrèges teeshirt, a Guy Laroche blouse or a Saint Laurent dress are no longer the stuff of which dreams are made. The cachet has worn

a bit thin – the price designers have had to pay in order to keep in business.

What has helped make French fashion is the average Frenchwoman's attitude to clothing. She has an inborn interest in and respect for fashion, coupled with a lack of puritan reservations about looking good.

The Paris **Opera House** (above) is equally well known for its sense of style. It faces the wide Avenue de l'Opéra like an Italian palazzo, a classical building of antiquity and a wedding cake all rolled into one monumental edifice.

The man who designed it, Charles Garnier, wanted something lavish and opulent to suit the Second Empire. His creation, located on a square roughly the size of an entire city block, took 14 years to build and opened its doors in 1875.

No modern building could be so lavish with its interior space as this vast monument which covers more than a hectare (almost three acres). The stage is big enough for 450 actors, but the auditorium can barely seat 2,200 spectators. Occupying a large area are the marble lobbies

and the great marble and onyx staircase. This is its true glory on gala nights, when the Republican Guards in dazzling uniforms and shiny metal helmets line the elegant steps in gleaming rows.

The Opéra's ceiling was a source of controversy some years ago, when the late Minister of Culture, André Malraux, announced plans for its redecoration. He had invited Russian painter Marc Chagall to decorate the ceiling in any way he wished. This caused great consternation in music circles, with serious opera-goers worrying that the unconventional artist would produce something totally unsuitable. But, when the brightly coloured Slavic dream ceiling was unveiled, even critics had to admit that it lightened the heavily ornate plush and gilt Opéra interior.

Streets around the Opéra are named after composers of the past, such as Auber and Glück, and the nearby Olympia hall features pop groups and French rock stars. Yet this is not a music lover's haunt, but the busiest shopping area in Paris, with the city's two most popular department stores, Galeries Lafayette and Le Printemps, just behind the Opéra.

However, music is on offer at other Paris venues, such as the concert halls, the churches and the *caves* or cellar halls, especially on the Left Bank. The range, from operetta and chamber music to folksongs and ballads, is wide for a nation which confesses to be unmusical.

Only occasionally has France excelled in classical music, unlike its neighbours Germany and Italy. It has rarely treated its composers with great respect. Berlioz, for example, died a poor and forgotten man. Debussy was hardly more fortunate; the audience shouted about the orchestra 'tuning their instruments' and not getting down to playing during the première of one of his works in 1902. Nevertheless there has been a recent revival of interest in opera. Although there was always a number of provincial opera companies in France, today their ranks are swelling. In the northwestern city of Nancy, for example, the civic opera company has been totally renovated, and is attracting loyal support from the citizens.

The **Louvre** (left), now one of the world's greatest museums, began as a fortress in 1200 and was built up over the centuries into one of the world's largest palaces.

Today's museum visitors are not the only commonfolk to have roamed through its vast halls. When the court moved to Versailles in the 17th century, shops and artists' studios were set up in the once-grand rooms. The entire palace might have been torn down, so deeply did it fall into disrepair, if it had not been for Napoleon who instructed that work should recommence on the building.

The museum first opened to the public in 1793 and over the years a number of important acquisitions have filled its six departments. Among the most loved of the Louvre's estimated 400,000 items are the *Victory of Samothrace*, the winged statue which resembles the prow of a ship; the delicate *Vénus de Milo* Greek sculpture; and Leonardo da Vinci's enigmatic *Mona Lisa*.

The calm Tuileries Gardens along one side of the Louvre, a relief after the rich treasure house, were designed in the 17th century by one of France's best landscape artists, Le Nôtre, and are a very model of the harmonious and formal French garden.

Its most breathtaking vista, the Triumphal Way, sweeps past the Place de la Concorde and up the Champs-Élysées to the **Arc de Triomphe** (below left). Nothing could be more noble than this triumphal arch, planned by Napoleon in the 1800s, to honour the French army. Carved in its massive stone are the names of victorious battles and generals, and monumental sculptures commemorate epic episodes in the life of the French. The finest, depicting the departure of the army in 1792 and known as *La Marseillaise*, symbolizes the Motherland spreading her wings and inciting her sons to fight. Beneath this epic arch is the Tomb of the Unknown Soldier with its continuously burning flame, a homage dating from World War 1.

Although the Champs-Élysées is now a commerical thoroughfare jammed with airline offices, car showrooms and tourist cafés, it slips back into its grandeur on July 14, French Independence Day. The tricolour, the French national flag, lines the long avenue and waves like a proud sail from the centre of the Arc.

One favourite among Paris' many bridges is the **Pont Alexandre III** (below). Against the stern-looking Invalides, it might appear a fussy piece of kitsch. But to saunter

along the graceful lamp-posted span with gilded statues in each corner is to return to the days of the *Belle Epoque*. Built at the end of the 19th century, this bridge evokes an era of lavishness and exuberance, when engineers would think nothing of placing groups of cupids and lions on a 107-metre (350-foot) metal-girded bridge. It is named after Tsar Alexander III of Russia and was built as a symbol of Franco-Russian entente.

The Paris Flea Market, the **Marché aux Puces** (left), is like a North African souk where everything is on hand for the intrepid buyer. Located in the north of the city just beyond the Porte de Clignancourt, it is a vast maze of stalls in alleys and courts, selling yesterday's antiques, today's junk and tomorrow's curios.

Bargain-hunters are warned not to expect too much from the varied treasure chest. Dealers have become knowledgeable about market prices since the 1920s, when antiques could be ferreted out for a song, and prices now parallel those in Paris shops. However, it is still possible to stumble across a delightful trinket in the jumble of goods.

Today a large part of the fun at the Puces involves people-watching. There are tourists and vagabonds, collectors and young couples searching for furniture, elegant Left Bank antique shop owners and junk dealers.

However, the best vantage point for observing life is from a café. And even in districts like the Beaubourg, with its modern snack bars, business thrives for the **everyday local café** (below).

These are often a bastion of the small businessman, with the boss behind the counter of 'zinc' and his wife at the till in a corner. The waiters move with harassed gait from bar to table, balancing glasses on an aluminium tray and eyeing customers for tips. Bills are usually 50 per cent more at an outside table than at the bar, but the real café-goer leaves the front row to the tourists, as it is a target for street vendors and buskers. He sits, preferably in the back, nursing an espresso coffee, a beer, a 'blanc sec' (glass of dry white wine) or a 'coup de rouge' (glass of red wine). He is watching or reading and not drinking seriously; for the real drinking is done at the bar, often starting early in the morning. Anyone who wishes to use the telephone at the bar can purchase special 'jetons' or tokens from the cashier. Also for sale are stamps, postcards and cigarettes and cigars.

The Georges Pompidou National Centre for Art and Culture, commonly known as the **Centre Beaubourg** (above) because of the area in which it is built, was opened in 1977 and has become the city's cultural playground.

This futuristic complex of concrete, glass and piping, an Anglo-Italian design, has transformed the neighbourhood from a seedy wasteland to a fashionable district. It is the pride of forward-thinking Paris architects and culture leaders, but the distress of the conservatives and the old people who once lived in this quarter.

When the ambitious project was being planned in 1969, President Georges Pompidou hoped it would make Paris the centre of the art world, the position it held before World War 2 and later lost to New York. Although it is still too early to determine whether Beaubourg has helped to repair Paris' sagging art reputation, it has made its cultural life a little more lively.

Musicians, sword swallowers and clowns now stage impromptu events in the outside plaza. A multi-arts centre is housed behind the exposed pipes and girders, with a transparent escalator weaving diagonally up its outside. Most of the city's modern art collection can now be found here, as well as a plastic arts section with permanent and temporary exhibitions. There is also a public library with half a million volumes, language laboratories, music cassettes, and over 150,000 carousels containing slides of the world's works of art.

And that's not all. A centre for *avant-garde* music, the Institute of Acoustical-Music Research and Coordination under composer-conductor Pierre Boulez, has engineers, sociologists and linguists exploring new musical directions. Another department, the Industrial Design Centre, has featured ski equipment and pavement café furniture among its numerous exhibitions.

There is no better contrast between new and old Paris than the futuristic Centre Beaubourg and Montmartre's nostalgic **Place du Tertre** (right).

Montmartre, too, was the artistic quarter, even before the late 1800s, when the white-domed Sacré-Coeur was constructed. Life was cheap on the 'Butte', as Parisians call the 130-metre (430-foot) rooftop of Paris, and the living was easy in the tree-filled village.

Many artists set up their easels in this little village, among them Renoir, Toulouse-Lautrec and Utrillo. Renoir's *Girl on a Swing* was painted here and so were some of the melancholic landscapes of Utrillo. However, the artist who did the most for Montmartre was Picasso who lived here at the beginning of his career. It was in Montmartre that he painted a canvas that was to change the course of art: *Les Demoiselles d'Avignon* was the first important work of Cubism.

Times have changed and today's artists congregating at the Place du Tertre prefer to specialize in commercial canvases mainly for tourists. And yet, the charm of Montmartre, the cobblestone streets and windmills, is just a few steps away.

Some say Montmartre, which was not annexed to Paris until 1860, derives its name from 'Mont des Martyrs', the spot where the first Bishop of Paris, St Denis, was executed. However, today's scholars trace its name back to 'Mons Mercurii', the hill of Mercury on which a pagan temple was situated. The nightlife of Montmartre is not as wild as at the turn of the century, when can-can dancers and absinthe drinkers turned night to day.

The Palace of Versailles was the nerve-centre of France for more than 100 years, from the reign of Louis XIV to the French Revolution.

The **Hall of Mirrors** (left) is among the most lavish of the reception rooms built during Louis XIV's rule. In his day, this 75-metre (246-foot) hall was filled with carpets and orange trees. The magnificent mirrors stretching along one side reflected an elite court at play, attired in the best silks and satins of the land.

This enormous 17th century palace with around 100 hectares (250 acres) of gardens and parklands was the pride and joy of Louis XIV. It was his bold decision to create Versailles from scratch on a marshy, hilly site outside Paris. His motive was to have the court in one place so he could solidify his power, and he personally supervized the construction project.

The actual building was the responsibility of architects Le Vau and Mansart. Their idea was to create a sense of grandeur by building in majestic proportions.

The interior decoration, the work of Le Brun, is not as over-rich as it would first appear to be. His approach was to decorate a room on geometric lines, and to give the sumptuous feeling through the use of the finest materials.

The **gardens of Versailles** (below) were laid out by Le Nôtre, France's most famous landscape gardener, and are a masterpiece of formal flowerbeds and parklands, fountains and huge lakes. Allegorical statues on vast basins facing the palace depict French rivers, while elsewhere an English garden, a rustic watermill and farm, and a hunting park can be found. Versailles has also had its critics. Saint-Simon noted: 'The magnificence of the gardens is amazing, but to make the smallest use of them is disagreeable . . . the broken stones on the paths burn one's feet, yet without them one would sink into sand or the blackest mud. Who could not help being repelled at the violence done to Nature?'

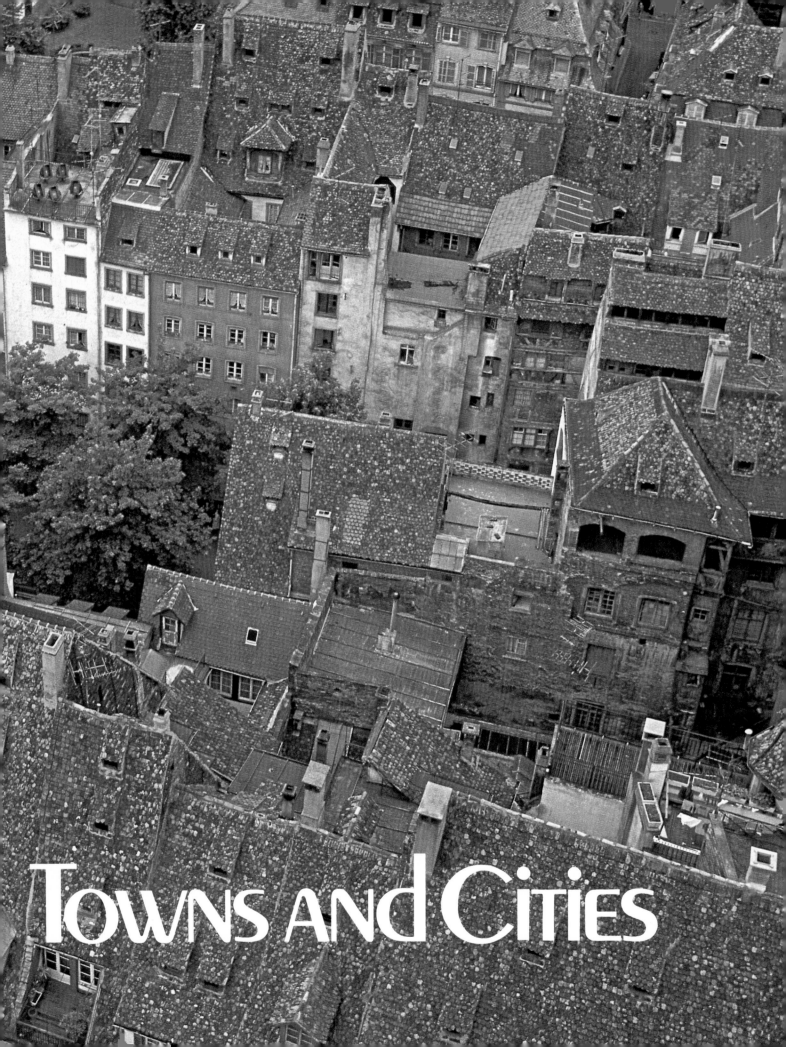

TOWNS AND CITIES

'A harmonious sowing of living cities, prosperous and equal'
Alain Griotteray

This is the way most French would like to regard their cities. They emerged from World War 2 with a deep desire to rebuild their war-torn country in a balanced way. The hope was that Paris would not prosper at the expense of the other towns and cities.

With 'regional development' as their battlecry, planners and politicians have been trying to enliven slumbering provincial centres over the last few decades. Consequently, cities like Lyon and Bordeaux are now flourishing and prosperous places.

France is made up of all kinds of human clusterings. There are sprawling cities like **Strasbourg** (preceding pages) and secretive walled towns like Carcassonne. Some, like Chartres, are centred around a cathedral, while others hug the walls of a castle to which they owe their existence. Many are precariously perched on cliffs and several nestle in valleys.

Each glistening concrete jungle, dusty, gold-stoned town, and village with thatched roofs is a dynamic self-contained community. Together they add up to a formidable treasure house of architectural delights which cannot fail to impress.

The gigantic and breathtaking **Cathedral of Chartres** (above) positively eclipses the agricultural town which nestles around it. Even from afar, the cathedral's graceful spires soar above the flat wheatfields of the Beauce plains southwest of Paris.

All around the cathedral are delightful old houses and streets with names like the Rue au Lait (Milk Street). The cathedral seems to look down on them like a protecting angel, evoking a sense of awe rare in these times.

A masterpiece of medieval architecture, Chartres cathedral is also a testament to the religious fervour of another era. Rich and poor alike helped to rebuild it after it was almost destroyed by fire in 1194. The reconstruction took a mere 30 years, extremely fast for the times.

The cathedral is architecturally astonishing in that the walls are not solid stone but filled with stained glass. The light inside is staggering; it filters through the famous windows, some of them 700 years old, and turns the stone floor into a kaleidoscope of colour, including the renowned 'Chartres blue'.

Rouen (right), now an important port in Normandy, has not forgotten its past. The cathedral, which dates back to the 11th century, was devastated by fire in 1200. One of Rouen's famous treasures is the *Gros Horloge* or Great Clock, an enormous timepiece with a single hand marking the hours on a red, blue and gold background. The signs of the week appear on the lower half of the face, and another element shows the phases of the moon. It was located in a belfry until 1525, when the people of Rouen insisted it be moved to a more prominent site. The clock arch straddles a long street which leads to the Place du Vieux-Marché, the square where Joan of Arc was burned alive in 1431.

Travelling eastward through Joan of Arc's native Lorraine and into Alsace, there is a procession of tiny villages; **Ribeauvillé** (above), with a population of 5,000, seems a giant among pygmies. This long and narrow town, famous for Traminer and Riesling wines, is dominated by its main street. A perfect setting for a parade, Ribeauvillé comes alive each year on 'Pfifferday', a traditional Alsatian festival. Inhabitants and visitors form a large procession to sing and dance along the street, passing under the 13th-century Butcher's Tower belfry and to emerge in the main square for free wine.

The joyous event dates back to the days when workers in nearby vineyards and travelling musicians gathered in Ribeauvillé to pay their respects to the great lords of the region, the Ribeaupierres.

Alsatian towns have a more German feel than those in other parts of France, with pointed roofs and timbered houses. One of the most charming is Colmar, where little waterways wend through narrow streets. This delightfully quaint town was the birthplace of Baron Haussmann, who demolished the narrow roads of Paris and laid out the wide boulevards so familiar today.

Vézelay (right), in Burgundy, has a completely different feel from Alsatian towns. It sits solidly on a hill, a town of stone that appears unchanged since the Middle Ages. From afar, Vézelay and its church look like one unit, a tight group of buildings in a surprisingly rural setting. And yet the complex feels as if it belongs just there, as if it merely rose from the stones and the earth into its present shape. From a distance, there are no iron girders or prefabricated blocks to spoil its timelessness.

Enter Vézelay on foot, struggling up steep streets, past houses tightly pressed together, towards the top of the hill. There, with the town spread around it like a skirt, is the Basilica of Ste-Madeleine, one of the famous pilgrimage centres of France.

Compared with Chartres or Notre-Dame, this is a sombre church. It is constricted and geometrical, long and vertical. The impression is of stone, not stained glass, of severe arches and not ornamental extravagances. Inside, white and dark stone give detail to the arches. There are wonderful sculptures of animals and peasants at work on top of many of the columns, which give a glimpse of life in medieval France. There is also a representation of 'Good' versus 'Bad'.

Vézelay has been a religious centre for more than 1,000 years, since Benedictine monks built a church on this slope in the 9th century. The Basilica and its name date back to the 11th century, when relics of Mary Magdalene were brought to Vézelay.

The town situated on the pilgrimage routes of Jerusalem and Santiago de Compostela, became a vital stopping off spot for two centuries. This seemingly secluded church and town was the rendezvous of saints and kings, of Thomas à Becket, St Bernard, Richard the Lionheart and France's religious king, St Louis.

Visitors to Vézelay should not miss nearby Avallon, a fine example of a medieval fortified town. It is located on high land and surrounded by ramparts, which date back to the time of Louis XIV; he used Avallon as a military base and sold the ramparts to the people when he decided the town was no longer of military significance.

The area all around Vézelay is drenched in history, full of artistic and architectural treasures and abundant in food and wine. Many of its towns have given their names to wines known the world over: Gevrey-Chambertin, Beaujolais, Beaune, Chablis, Clos de Vougeot, Château-Chinon. Some are no more than suggestions of villages, like Volnay or Vosne-Romanée. Beaune, however, is a contemporary town except for its ramparts and Renaissance Hospices.

Also fascinating are the religious centres which once proliferated in this region in the 9th to 13th centuries. Some remains form the basis for small towns, while others are hardly more than ruins. The Cistercian Abbey of Cîteaux, the home of St Bernard, has nearly disappeared from today's map. The Abbey of Fontenay, near the small town of Montbard, has been restored but it is only a museum and not the centre of a contemporary town. The Romanesque church at Tournus, one of the earliest of its kind, stands in a small, cobblestoned town on the Saône river. And all that remains of the Abbey of Cluny, whose church was once the largest Christian worshipping place and an important centre in the Middle Ages, is a collection of near ruins.

The peaceful-looking city of **Orléans** (left) was the scene of great battles between the English and French crowns. In the early 1400s the English, with the Burgundy nobles as their allies, had almost divided up France among themselves. Orléans was one of the last cities still held by the French king, and Lord Salisbury arrived there in 1428.

The river banks were covered with Lord Salisbury's trenches of earth and wood, and garrisons of about 450 men were stationed in strongholds along the quais. Both sides shouted at each other across the trenches for more than five long months in a stalemate broken by the arrival of Joan of Arc. Using a bridge of boats to help her cross the river, she drove the English away and delivered Orléans to the king.

The Orléans of today bears little resemblance to the town Joan wrested from the English and their Burgundian allies. The main centre has been rebuilt as air raids virtually destroyed many of its buildings and museums during World War 2. Also, the cathedral, with its lovely centre spire was constructed after the Protestants destroyed the original during the religious wars of the 16th century.

The River Loire is 300 metres (330 yards) wide when it reaches Orléans, a city now known for its roses, and it is crossed by a number of bridges. One of these, the Pont George V, was considered unsafe by the inhabitants when it was erected in 1760. The king's mistress, Mme de Pompadour, crossed it herself to prove that it would not fall down. This caused a local wit to remark: 'Our bridge is strong. It has borne France's heaviest burden.' Sadly for Mme de Pompadour, he was referring to the extravagant financial burden she placed on the French people.

27

The town of **Amboise** (below) has grown up around the ancient castle after which it is named, crawling up the banks of the Loire to the vast chimney-potted château.

Visitors to Amboise can wander through its small museum, pause at its fountain by surrealist artist Max Ernst, continue past charming houses, some more than 500 years old, and visit the lovely Clos Lucé, a 15th-century manor house which is now a museum devoted to Leonardo da Vinci.

The château is in private hands, so the views are restricted mainly to the sights outside. There is a magnificent terrace inside the castle walls with a panorama of the Loire Valley countryside. This was virtually an enclosed courtyard, in times gone by, with buildings surrounding it on all sides.

The two enormous towers, the Tour Hurtault and the Tour des Minimes, can be reached by mounting interior ramps so wide that even cars could drive up them. Up on the ramparts is the beautiful Chapelle St-Hubert, decorated to resemble the home of St Hubert, patron of hunters.

In the late 15th century, Amboise became a great palace, the Versailles of its day. Charles VIII loved Amboise and spent much time and money transforming the original fortress into a splendid royal centre. Leonardo da Vinci, who later came to Amboise, was so attracted by the town he asked to be buried there.

However, Amboise's fortunes changed in 1560, when a large public execution took place in the castle. Around 1,500 religious plotters were slaughtered while the royal family looked on.

Not all ancient castles have given birth to thriving modern towns. The **Château de Duingt** (below) in the French Alps, a residence since the 11th century and rebuilt in the 17th except for its cylindrical tower, is still quite isolated from the rest of humanity. Located on a peninsula in Lake Annecy, a stone's throw from Switzerland, it commands a wonderful view of one of France's most beautiful alpine lakes. Close by is the charming town of Annecy with its narrow streets and quiet canals.

Bordeaux (above) is a city that has become great again. A thriving wine industry and busy commercial port have helped to make this southwestern city one of France's most important modern centres.

Bordeaux has seen many changes over the centuries. During the Roman occupation it became an important trading centre and its new citizens started to plant vineyards around their villas. Bordeaux was also prosperous during the 300 years of English domination. It was their base in France after Henry II of England married Eleanor of Aquitaine in 1152. Commerce expanded with English traders exporting large quantities of claret wine.

Much later, in the 18th century, France's trade with her West Indian and African colonies gave Bordeaux a new lease of life. But poor harvests and Napoleon's crusades marked the beginning of a period of decline, which even continued into the 20th century.

Bordeaux then became known as the least progressive large city in all of France. This sorry state of affairs did not change until the late 1950s, when Mayor Jacques Chaban-Delmas decided that this position must be reversed. He persuaded the government and Bordelais authorities to encourage new industry and, as a result, a huge complex with refineries and factories has grown up on the other side of the Garonne River, putting Bordeaux firmly on the international map again.

The most resplendent of today's French cities, second only to Paris, is **Lyon** (right). Rich enough to preserve its ancient quarters of cobbled streets and arcaded houses, it is a fine example of a thriving modern French city.

Lyon, the second largest city in France, with a population nearing 1.2 million, is prosperous because of the heavy manufacturing, chemical, textile and metallurgical industries based there. Lyon now looks very different from its appearance during its first renaissance, when it was the capital of the silk industry, filled with elegant town houses. The 20th-century transport system has made the cobblestone streets redundant, with underground trains, international airport, ring roads and fast motorways to link Lyon with the rest of the world.

The Lyonnais can point with civic pride to many parts of his city: for example, the Place des Terraux with its large fountain of four horses, or the Place Bellecour with its enormous statue of Louis XIV on horseback and wonderful restaurants and cafés. Lyon also has a flourishing opera house and an excellent museum of fine arts which contains priceless paintings, including Rembrandts and Van Goghs.

The museums of Lyon are a treat in themselves. One traces the history of dental surgery and another the evolution of fire-fighting. The Puppet Museum, in the grandiose 16th-century Hotel de Gadagne mansion, presents one of Lyon's most famous citizens – Guignol, hero of the French puppet theatre, who was created in Lyon in 1795.

However, it is only since the 1960s that Lyon has managed to become a modern international city. In recent history, it has been a satellite of Paris, with many of its large firms located in the French capital. Even the important bank named after Lyon, the Crédit Lyonnais, had moved its headquarters to Paris.

Now that it has gained some autonomy and has become more cosmopolitan, the people have lost some of the stuffiness for which they always have been criticized. The street scene is becoming more lively and open than before. Even the restaurants, which serve some of the best food in France, are becoming more aware of outside influences.

The immense Palace of the Popes still dominates the vista of the provençal city of **Avignon** (right), just as it did 500 years ago. However, a lively, sunny city has blossomed beneath its shadow.

Each summer, Avignon is host to a famous drama festival and international companies perform their works in the courtyard of the palace, bringing fresh new life to this rather stern building.

Avignon's history can be traced back to ancient times, but it was in the 14th century that it became truly glorious, an international capital and the centre of Christianity. It was at this time when Pope Clement V escaped from the intrigues of Rome and came to live in Avignon. Indeed he was the first of seven French Popes to do so. In 1348, the Church purchased Avignon, and the Palace of the Popes, with its labyrinth of halls and audience rooms, was developed and extended by a succession of Popes.

Sadly the bridge featured in the famous rhyme *Sur le Pont d'Avignon* is not fit to dance across today. Only four arches of its original 900-metre (980-yard) span survive.

Southwest of Avignon is one of the world's most startling architectural sights, **Carcassonne** (below). It is a massive fortified city with defensive walls and 54 towers. From afar, it looks the same as it did 600 years ago, when its newest parts were added.

However, Carcassonne was actually restored to its present dramatic glory in the 19th century. It had fallen into disrepair after the 17th century, when it had no military function to fulfil. The architect Viollet-le-Duc was asked to carry out the work, the world's first large-scale restoration of this kind.

Some walls can be traced back to the Romans in the 1st century BC, and towers built by the Visigoths, who captured Carcassonne in the 5th century, are still standing.

However, it was St Louis and his son, Philip the Bold, who were the architects of much of the present-day Carcassonne. Their building activities, which were completed in the 13th century, included the erection of many of the towers and the two strong castellated walls of fortification.

The city behind these formidable walls was intended to withstand any siege. There was ample room to store food and water supplies to last many months. A mint and a mill helped to make it virtually self-sufficient.

Although the wealthy capital of the Tarn region in the southwest, with industrial areas in its outlying districts, **Albi** (right) evokes another time and place. Today's tranquil ochre-red and pink town was the scene of bitter battles in the 13th century. These were between the Church of Rome and the heretic 'Cathares'.

Ste-Cécile, Albi's enormous cathedral, is a living reminder of this bloody time. It is actually a fortress, built by Bernard de Castanet, a 13th century bishop, who used it as a base from which to conduct a full-scale Inquisition.

Like this unique cathedral, the Episcopal Palace (Palais de la Berbie) was also built as a fortress. It now houses a fine collection of the works of the artist Henri de Toulouse-Lautrec, Albi's most famous citizen.

When Toulouse-Lautrec died in 1901, his mother gave his works to Albi. His birthplace, however, still belongs to his family, but visitors can see some parts of the house, as well as a collection of early sketches that show the origins of his creative genius.

The people of France

'This Frenchman, who takes so much pain to be orderly in his thinking and so little in his actions, this logician always torn by doubt . . . this imperial adventurer who loves nothing more than his hearth at home . . . this uncertain, unstable and contradictory people.'
Charles de Gaulle

More than 53,580,000 of these people so aptly described by their general and president are alive and well and living in France. Some are tall with blue Scandinavian eyes and others are stocky and of Latin origin. The Breton's French has a Welsh lilt, and the **Hérault farmer** (preceding pages) can sound as if he speaks a mixture of French, Provençal and Spanish.

As France becomes increasingly industrialized the horse is being replaced by the tractor, and the family-owned bistro by restaurant chains. However, one thing never changes – the quintessential Frenchness of the French. They are a nation of civilized hedonists, lovers of food and drink, and romance. They are the artists of everyday life, the people who can turn a mundane meal into a personal creation.

They are also very industrious with a healthy respect for their country and its traditions. They work hard to earn their livelihood and they play hard; put simply, their philosophy is *savoir vivre* – knowing how to live life and to live it well.

To see the making of pâté in a farmhouse in the **Charente** (below left), the area near Cognac, is to lose one's sense of time. Off the main roads and deep in the countryside, life often rolls on in the same old way. The horse can be seen working the field, the old can be dreaming in dusty squares, the women can be tending to their houses.

In universities and cities far from the farmhouse, yet another theory has emerged about French cuisine. The word is that French cooking derived not so much from the people themselves but from the Paris restaurants opened by chefs freed from châteaux kitchens by the French Revolution. However, at grassroots level, cooking in France is an art and skill that is passed from generation to generation, like old wives' tales or superstitions.

The secrets, if there are any, consist of two homilies: the balance of time and money and the use of fresh produce. Older Frenchwomen can be adamant about the superiority of their time-tested pots over modern equipment. Some won't even use a whisk to turn egg whites into meringue. A new crêpe pan can fill them with horror. And they insist a cook can ruin a sauce merely by one small change of arm movement.

The meals produced by these *maîtresses de maison* are testaments of their abilities. Strict rules exist for the laying of the table, the decorating of each dish, the content of each meal. The seating of guests, especially when clergy are at the table, is carefully thought out.

Most regions of France have always had a thriving local cuisine based on the produce of the area. A cult of regional cooking has sprung up since the advent of the car, with partisans praising one or another provincial restaurant. Regional specialities include Brittany's *homard à l'amoricaine*, lobster in a garlic, tomato and wine sauce and named after the ancient name of Brittany, Armorica; Normandy's *tripes à la mode de Caen*, tripe in calvados, said to have been eaten by William the Conqueror; Languedoc's *cassoulet*, bean stew with goose or duck, pork or lamb; Burgundy's *boeuf bourguignon*, beef stewed in wine; and Marseille's *bouillabaisse*, fish stew including up to 20 different types of fish and shellfish cooked with tomatoes, garlic and onions.

A recent trend favours less highly seasoned dishes and fewer rich sauces. It is called the *Cuisine Minceur*, or *Nouvelle Cuisine*, and is based on combining taste with fewer calories and less cholesterol.

The cooking is still highly flavoured along the south coast of France, and even local vendors in **Marseille** (right) sell varieties of spiced olives. The choice can range from Greek olives to olives in *herbes de provence* or in garlic. The peppers and pimentos add a dash of colour to home-cooked dishes, and the sausage can be added to a stew.

Shopping for food in France is an event in itself; traditional specialist shops have not been edged out by the supermarkets. A lot of time and patience, plus a straw bag and a strong arm, are needed to carry home the bottles of water and wine, the kilos of fruit and vegetables.

Sausages sold by stall-owners are in a bewildering array in the *charcuterie*, the culinary treasurehouse that can provide a beautiful and tasty cooked meal. They often hang in long ropes from the ceilings, in all shapes, colours and sizes. Some are *ménages pur porc*, made only of pork; others are flecked pork chipolatas. Delicate white *boudin blanc*, white pudding, is laid on the counters alongside pâtés of varying textures and tastes, roast chicken, cold salmon and sliced ham.

mille-feuilles. Other specialities are sold at various times of the year, like the huge highly decorated coffee or chocolate *buche de noël* cake loaves for Christmas.

Elegant French restaurants like **Maxim's** (below) in Paris are sought after by chefs longing to work on the staff, by maîtres-d'hôtel at the pinnacle of their profession, and by discerning lovers of gourmet cooking.

These restaurants create an ambience in which mere eating is transformed into a sophisticated and refined occasion. Impeccable china, linen, silver cutlery and crystal glasses adorn the tables. Each customer is discreetly served by a number of waiters in black tie, and the elegantly attired clientele need not flicker an eyelid to get attention. The offerings are the visual and culinary masterpieces of the French cuisine.

This gastronomic opulence belies the fact that eating habits have been changing in France. The two-hour lunch break has been replaced by a quick meal in a snack bar or café. Frozen foods are creeping on to French tables, with over four million households now owning a deep freeze. Sales of yogurt and cheese are increasing while those of bread, potatoes, fresh vegetables and fruit are falling.

A highpoint in the French sporting calendar is the **Tour de France** (right). It is a mammoth bicycle race around the perimeter of the country which starts at the end of June and goes on for an aching 25 days.

The event, which began in 1903, has a 4,800 km (3,000 mile) course which changes each year. Nevertheless competitors always have to contend with the heat of the south and the tortuous mountain passes of the Alps.

Those cheering supporters who line the route are usually bicycle fanatics themselves, if of a more gentle variety. In

There are probably as many **boulangeries** (above) in France as there are cafés. The French go to the baker once a day, and not to socialize. It is the only way to make sure that their daily loaf is fresh. The long crusty bread is made of flour that does not keep – hence the delicate texture – and most bakers produce bread twice a day. The aroma of baking is one of the wonderful smells of France: it wafts from the ovens, through the shops and into the streets.

Bread, served without butter, is a mainstay of the French meal. The *bâtard* (pictured) is thicker and shorter than the *baguette*, a wand-like loaf of crusty bread. The *ficelle* is extremely thin and very long, and lucky the person who gets home without it breaking in two. The *pain de campagne*, made of heavy dough, can keep for a few days and is a good accompaniment for a meal of red wine, sausage and cheese. There are also the round *couronne* breads and one with crunchy pieces of dough called an *épi*.

If the customer does not want a whole loaf, he is welcome to purchase a section of bread. *Le quart de baguette* – a quarter of a *baguette* – is a not uncommon request, with bakers slicing the loaf on the wood counter with a sharp, long knife.

The *boulangerie* also sells *croissants*, crescent-shaped pastry, or the richer more expensive version called *croissant au beurre*. Also on offer are a bevy of breaded delights, such as *petit pain au chocolat*, a delicate roll with a stick of dark chocolate baked in the centre, and *petit pain au raisin*, a delicious baked combination of raisins, dough and custard rolled into a circular shape.

Some *boulangeries* leave cake-baking to the *pâtisserie*, the specialist cake shop, where the fare is overwhelming. There are *tartes aux fruits*, *petits fours*, luscious *éclairs* and flaky

recent years the bicycle has become a popular means of getting around in France, with 15 million of them wending through the 17 million private cars on the roads.

A less energetic sport than bicycling, perhaps, but a very popular one with young and old is boules or **pétanque** (above). It is a form of bowls, played throughout southern France in village squares or almost anywhere in the open air. Serious participants can join a national *pétanque* club, located in the town of Lyon.

The French were never very sporty as a nation, but they have become more so in recent years, with almost one tenth of the population now belonging to one sporting club or another. Soccer is the favourite sport, with more than 1.3 million amateur footballers. But tennis and horse riding, once the sports of the rich, are becoming very popular. So, too, is sailing, which has only recently emerged on the scene. Sailor Eric Tabarly is among France's handful of internationally known sports personalities. The country has not generally excelled in world class competitions. Accordingly, more sporting facilities have been provided in recent years, including stadiums, gymnasiums and swimming pools.

In Sauveterre de Rouergue, Aveyron, **two elderly men** (right) are taking the sun in their own way. Like them, thousands of old-age pensioners are being gradually helped out of the isolation and poverty that can come with what the French call 'the third age'.

The new official approach to the elderly is to help old single people of limited means to remain in their homes, by providing home help and clubs for the elderly. The previous policy was to house them in state institutions, where many felt like prisoners or helpless children.

These two men, like all citizens, are eligible for a minimum pension in their old age. There is an earnings-related scheme which began in 1945 but which is only finally beginning to yield results. However, the people who were self-employed or who missed out on paying contributions do not qualify. They get subsidies to help pay the rent, and medical and psychiatric services that are free or at low cost. But the government only gives them 1,000 francs a month to cover their costs, which is not a large amount. Many over-65s, who make up about 13 per cent of the population, are better off. However, even the French government recognizes that much work remains to be done.

The girl sweeps her hair under her delicate white headdress, places her cross around her neck and puts on her local costume for the **Festival de Nîmes** (above).

In the past decade or so, the younger generation of French women have been railing against the traditional pattern of a Frenchwoman's life. Some now question the entire premise upon which marriage is based. They have smaller families; the average family has shrunk to less than two children. Although, as in the past, they are still getting married they are also getting divorced. In the 1970s, girls like this one began to make an impact in politics and other professions. Abortion was made legal, and inequalities in divorce, property ownership and employment were rectified by new laws.

Despite these radical changes, the Frenchwoman has not altered all that much. She still regards herself as equal, but different, from men. She wants feminism and femininity, like Simone Veil, the elegant and brilliant lawyer who rose to become French Minister of Health and President of the European Parliament in Brussels. Mme Veil summed it up a few years ago: 'It's important to present a well-groomed front without in any way trying to be a pin-up.'

Hundreds of **fishermen** (above) still sail out of ports in Brittany in wooden ships, trying to make a living from catching mackerel, sole, whiting and skate in the English Channel and the Atlantic.

These fishermen, and those of neighbouring Normandy, can still practise their trade, but they are being threatened, they say, by the big efficient enterprises of France and other European countries. Foreign competition, the 320 km (200 mile) fishing limit, rising costs and falling prices have added up to what many feel is a danger to their livelihood.

In recent years, these independent fishermen have banded together to bring attention to their plight. They have gone to court to fight companies dumping industrial waste in the waters and ruining their catch. They have blockaded Channel ports.

The Bretons on their lonely jagged northern peninsula seem almost a race apart from the rest of the French. They trace their roots back to the Celts, some of whom came from the British Isles and others who were here since 6 BC. The Celts are the people who gave this region the name of Bretagne, or little Britain. Their lineage also traces back to a probably Iberian people who left mysterious Stonehenge in Britain and the parallel archaeological treasure, Carnac,

with its famous standing stones, in Brittany.

These people of France's Celtic country have not lost their unique identity. They have their own folklore and myths woven into their poetry and songs, and their belief in the supernatural is attributed by historians to their awe of the sea. They are still a religious people, and shrines can be found all over the countryside, with each town seeming to have its own favourite saint. Every year, there are hundreds of 'pardons' or religious pilgrimages and festivals with the women in their traditional starched lace headdress and the men also in local costume. Once the rites of mass and processions are over, there is exuberant folk dancing and singing of local songs. Many visitors throng to Brittany especially to see these colourful festivals, steeped in Breton legend.

Although French has been the official language of Brittany since the late 15th century when the region was annexed to France, the Breton language has not been forgotten, and in fact is now enjoying something of a revival. The question *'mat eo ar jeu ganit?'* has a deeper meaning for some in this mysterious land than 'how are things going?' These are the nationalist extremists, a small group of terrorists who fight to make Brittany a separate country.

The group's bomb attacks on buildings and even on the Palace of Versailles outside Paris have brought them some notoriety. But the average Breton does not support the violent means used to attain this goal. In fact, he does not even want to be independent of France, which he knows would amount to economic suicide for a rather poor region.

The **Basques** (right) are another group of French people who have a unique identity. They live on the slopes of the Pyrenees in the southwest tip of France, close to their fiery brothers in northern Spain.

They are an ancient people, whose origins are obscure. It has been suggested that some of their ways resemble those of the ancient Mayans and the Japanese. Theirs is a land of seven old provinces, three in France and four in Spain.

They are mainly farmers and fishermen, although some tend sheep on the marshy soil of the Landes, walking for miles on stilts. The majority of their houses are simple dwellings, often decorated with attractive and original peasant art. The Basque cuisine, with its seasoned dishes, has become popular in France. There is *jambon de Bayonne*, smoked ham from the town of Bayonne, and *civet de palombes*, stew made from woodcock. The Basques add pimento and ham to scrambled eggs (*piperade*) and eat trout and salmon from the mountain streams. The wines, often drunk in one long stream from a goatskin container, are Irouléguy and the white Herriko-Arnoa.

Their clothing has been adopted by other cultures with eagerness. The traditional beret can be seen far beyond the shores of France. The rope-soled shoes called espadrilles have become a regular item in many fashionable shops.

The Basques are a lively people, especially at festival times, when they perform their complicated dances with great gusto. This is often followed by singing and impromptu poetry recitals. A game of pelota, their national sport which resembles tennis or rackets, caps the events.

The French Basques rarely sympathize with their guerrilla brothers in Spain, where the majority of Basques live, and who have been fiercely fighting Spain for total independence. The French Basques, like the rest of the nation, are individualists gathered together in one country.

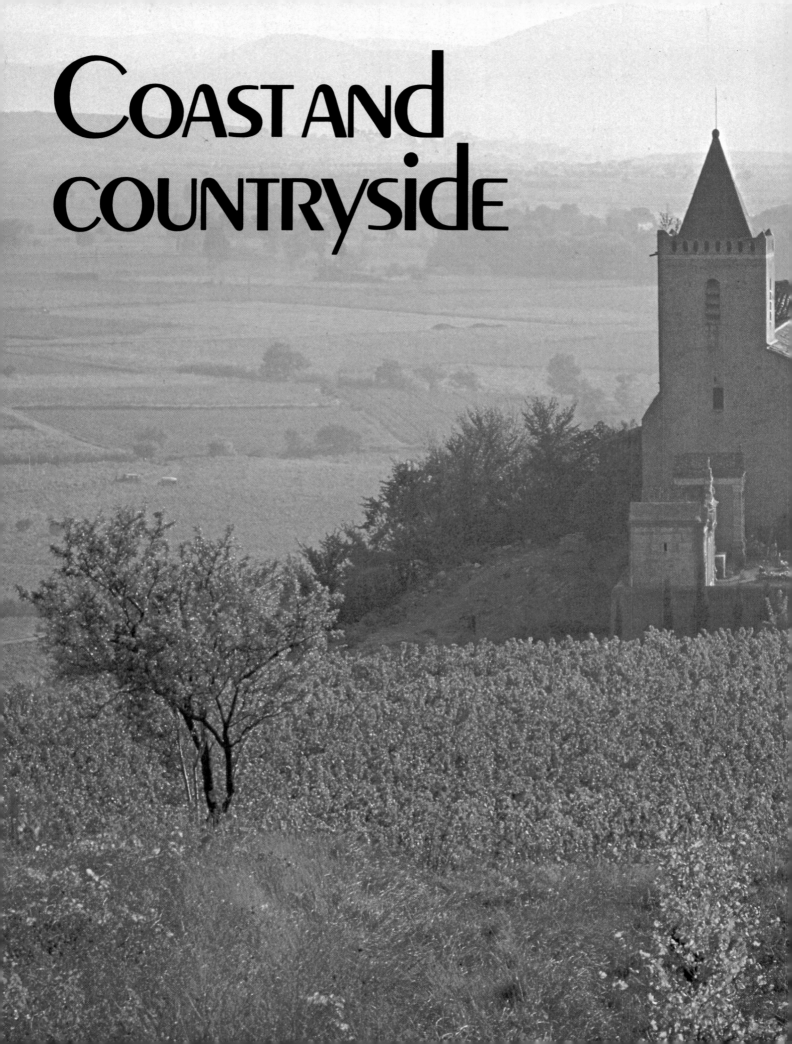

COAST AND COUNTRYSIDE

'Yet, who can help loving the land that has taught us
Six hundred and 85 ways to dress eggs?'
Thomas Moore

France is not a very large country, only 551,000 sq
km (212,700 square miles) including Corsica and
not even as big as Turkey. It is not as wealthy as
Germany, as densely populated as Holland, or quite
as picturesque as Italy. The beaches can be
unbearably crowded and the roads often jammed with
cars and their impatient drivers.

Nevertheless there is no doubt that France is a
most alluring nation with an enormous amount to
offer, including a rich and varied coast and
countryside.

Almost half of its borders are coastlines, ranging
from rocky northern Breton cliffs, along Atlantic
dunes, to Mediterranean coves. The countryside, criss-
crossed by about 27,000 rivers and streams, is a
patchwork of colours and textures. There are the flat
Beaune wheatfields and the soggy marshes of les
Landes, the snowcapped mountains of the Alps and
the dusty Midi terrains, the breathtaking Tarn river
gorges and the abundant **Hérault vineyards**
(preceding pages).

France is a land of three major river basins and
their uplands: the Garonne in the southwest, the
Seine in the north, and the rushing Rhône-Saône
in the southeast. The country was built up from many
small kingdoms and dukedoms over the centuries into
one sometimes unwieldy but definitely unified whole.

Some people refer to the territory in geographical
terms, such as the 'southwest' or the 'massif central'.
Others describe it in terms of the ancient provinces,
such as 'Périgord' or 'Languedoc'.

Today the French Republic is divided into three
types of political unit, whose names are also used to
describe an area of the land. There are 22 regions
which range from Alsace to Corsica and which bear a
certain resemblance to the old provinces. These are
divided into 95 départements, like Hérault in the
region of Languedoc-Roussillon, or the Jura in the
region of Franche-Comté. Then come the 36,400 or so
municipalities, some with less than 300 inhabitants.

The rich northwestern region of **Normandy** (right) is a
fisherman's paradise, where pike, perch, carp or trout can
be caught. Dieppe sole and steamed mussels in butter
(*moules à la marinière*), along with camembert and pont
l'evêque cheese, and the apple-based liqueur calvados, also
come from this region.

Normandy is named after the Normans, invaders from
Scandinavia who sailed up the Seine in Viking-type ships
burning and looting churches and monasteries. Their
leader Rollo agreed to be baptized, partly to make peace
with the Franks, and then he began restoring the religious
centres. This eventually led to the great Norman abbeys,
some of which can be seen today.

Normandy's **Mont-St-Michel** (far right) is one of the
wonders of France. It is a solitary outpost of Christianity;

the mountain of St Michael the Archangel, whose gilded
statue, complete with brandished sword, tips the slender
church spire.

Only one road leads to this granite mountain-island. A
long causeway, it traverses the mudbanks and quicksands
that separate this dramatic site from mainland France.

The base of the rock is as far as cars can go, and then
one has to climb the long single street which changes from
ramp to steep steps. Up through the ramparts, past the
parish church and other buildings built right into the rock,
and there is the abbey church, with its roof a full 900 steps
and 120 metres (400 feet) above the level of the sea.

The whole of Mt-St-Michel – village, churches, steps and
fortress – is a dizzying mixture of rock and building, of
nature and religion. The precipitous sheer cliffs, sometimes
the walls of buildings, give the feeling of dramatic
verticality.

A shrine in Celtic times and later the refuge of Christian
hermits, this site has been holy for centuries. Large forests
used to reach up to the mountain, until huge tidal waves

in the 8th century deluged the forests and severed the rock
from the mainland.

At this time St Michael himself is said to have appeared
in a vision to the bishop of the nearby town of Avranches,
ordering a small chapel to be built on the solitary rock.
This was erected here in AD 709, and was named 'St
Michael at Peril from the Sea'. Benedictine monks later
added the abbey and a large church, and everything was
completed by the 15th century. During the French
Revolution, the monks were dispersed and Mt-St-Michel
was later turned into a prison.

The terrifying grandeur of this lonely place, where the
wind howls through halls and around walls, is heightened
by the tide. It roars in at the amazing rate of 64 metres
(210 feet) a minute, withdrawing as far as 16km (10 miles)
at certain times of the year, and leaving deceivingly
smooth quicksands behind.

The varied coastline of Normandy has resorts and villages of all shapes and sizes, and the ancient fishing port of **Honfleur** (left) is among the most picturesque.

This town of about 9,000 inhabitants is a delightful place to visit. Fishermen continue to sail out of this tranquil port with its tall slate-roofed houses, spreading their nets in the waters of the Seine estuary and the English Channel beyond. 'The dearest of my dreams' is how the poet Baudelaire described Honfleur, where he stayed with his mother in her old age.

There is an impressive timber church which was built by the port carpenters in 1468, and there are old streets with charming names like *Rue de l'Homme-de-Bois*, Street of the Wooden Man. The town, with its excellent harbour for both power and sailing boats, has a interesting collection of Impressionist works in its museum, the Musée Eugène Boudin. In fact, Honfleur, with its remarkable quality of light, was a favourite setting for the Impressionist painters.

To the west are the grander resorts of Trouville and Deauville. Trouville, on the estuary of the Touques river, has also inspired Impressionist painters with its long wide beach and vast expanse of sea and sky.

Nearby Deauville is one of France's most chic resorts. It dates back to the 19th century, when the Duc de Mornay, the half brother of Napoleon III, put it on the map.

The 'season', from July to the end of August, is when the wealthy and famous descend on Deauville for their summer relaxation. They stroll along the 'Planches' – the long boardwalk kept as spic and span as the deck of a boat – and visit the famous casino and polo grounds. The *Grand Prix de Deauville*, a glittering horserace on the last Sunday in August, signals the end of the season.

Westward past the city of Cherbourg, with its busy ferry port, the coast becomes wild and lonely. This is a sharp contrast to the coastline east of Deauville and Honfleur, which goes past Étretat with its fabulous white cliffs and to Le Touquet, the resort with a lingering 1930s glamour and mile after mile of glorious sand and dunes.

And then there are the Normandy invasion beaches which stretch along 80 km (50 miles) of the coast and which saw the historic cross-Channel Allied invasion in June 1944 that led to the freeing of Europe. Museums, war memorials, military cemeteries and bunkers are tributes to that great landing.

The countryside of Normandy is also richly endowed with historic treasures. Most famous of these is the Bayeux Tapestry which consists of a long strip of linen embroidered in wool. Exhibited in the town of Bayeux, it shows in 58 scenes how William the Conqueror invaded England in 1066, and was made shortly after the Battle of Hastings.

Inland is a shrine for all medieval historians and lovers of church history. This is Le Bec-Hellouin, the great religious and cultural centre of the Middle Ages. Walking around the remains of the abbey, which was established in 1034, it is easy to imagine the time when many of Europe's most brilliant scholars and religious leaders were studying there. Among these was St Anselm, the philosopher and theologian, who became Archbishop of Canterbury in 1093 and died in 1109.

Not far away, perched on a high cliff overlooking the Seine, are the vast eerie ruins of Richard the Lionheart's monumental fortified castle, Château Gaillard. In its day, it commanded the whole countryside from behind thick walls and a moat.

The Loire Valley is France's fairytale country with peach trees, light rosé and delicious white wines, verdant countryside, and mile after mile of castles.

The château of **Chenonceaux** (below) is the jewel in the crown. Built on a bridge across the river Cher, it is one of the most delicate and graceful of the Loire châteaux.

From the day it was constructed by a collector of taxes in the 16th century, the château has been the prized dwelling for many owners. Among these were a king's mistress, Diane de Poitiers; two widowed Queens, Catherine de' Medici and Louise de Lorraine; and Claude Dupin and his wife, the hostess of famous literary and political gatherings.

Life at Chenonceaux has been varied over the centuries. There were flamboyant receptions, followed by prayers and nuns, and then the witty salons frequented by Lord Chesterfield and Voltaire. In World War 1, the château was used as a hospital for injured soldiers.

The French poet Charles Péguy claimed that there were 120 stately châteaux along the length of the majestic Loire river. This may involve poetic licence, but there is certainly a long procession of these magnificent buildings to be found here.

Some of these châteaux were royal palaces, owned by the king of the day. The most imposing of these centres of courtly life is Chambord.

More a castle than a Renaissance royal palace is Chinon. This is a long building composed of three fortresses separated by moats, the castle where Joan of Arc was introduced to Charles VII.

Others in this rich architectural parade were built by private citizens. Villandry, a Renaissance castle, was the creation of François I's secretary of state, Jean le Breton, while Chaumont, with grim pointed towers, owes its existence to the counts of Amboise.

Although most of these feudal fortresses, castles and stately homes look like palaces fit for any princess, the massive château of Ussé is the one which has gone down in literary history. Its fortified towers, turrets and chimneys are the supposed setting for *The Sleeping Beauty*, the famous fairytale written by Charles Perrault.

The Dordogne River meanders through the historic province of Périgord, southwest of the Loire Valley, and a much more rural area.

Castelnaud (above), with its square keep and round towers, is one of the most appealing castles in this region. Perched on a rocky hill above a village of stone houses, it looks out on hills and woods, watermills and farmhouses.

Castelnaud was an important English stronghold during the Hundred Years War between France and England. The English remained in the castle while the French tried hard to besiege it using the fortress at Beynac as a base.

In recent years, the English have returned to the Dordogne, buying up its stone houses and cottages. The French wryly refer to the region as 'English France', so populated has it become by the British.

A large part of the Dordogne's appeal is that it epitomizes most of the good things of rural France. **Women wash clothes** (right) in the quiet river, which moves imperceptibly through the valley. The cuisine – *pâté de foie gras*, truffles, *pintade* or guinea-fowl – is renowned. And the small inns and tiny towns, the exquisite pink limestoned cottages and villages built of red sandstone, make this a most enchanting place.

The **Gorges du Tarn** (below), the Gorges of the Tarn river, offer some of the most magnificent views in inland France. This is a forbidding part of the country, with more than 48 km (30 miles) of gorges and canyons in the limestone mountains.

Not many people live here. Visitors hardly ever came before the tortuous mountain road was constructed through the region. Now this awesome land with its rocky valleys and pitted cliffs has become a holiday paradise.

Pot-holers are attracted to the area and many search for rock specimens in underground rivers. Canoeists and sailing enthusiasts set out from bases along the Tarn's riverbanks, moving along the swift river through the deep gorges. Fishermen and hunters practise their sports in the rushing streams and on the hillsides.

The country westward is mountainous, with twisting subterranean rivers and gorges, and contains one of the most spectacular sights in France. This is the village of **Rocamadour** (right), a collection of buildings and dwellings which seem to cling to the side of a sheer cliff.

Rocamadour today has the reputation of being both a tourist trap and a religious pilgrimage centre. Its name derives from the remains of an unknown man discovered here in the 12th century. The tale spread that he was a Christian hermit who fled there from persecutions following Christ's crucifixion, and he received the name St Amadour. After reports of miracles, Rocamadour began to attract pilgrims from all over Europe in the Middle Ages.

Despite its fortifications and unlikely location, the little village was often plundered during various wars and the hermit's remains were destroyed. Fortunately it was carefully rebuilt in the early 19th century.

It is impossible not to be impressed by the spectacular beauty of the French Alps. Some of the world's best ski resorts are in this area including Chamonix, Megève, Courchevel and Val-d'Isère. There are glimpses of snowpeaked mountains like Mont Blanc, and wonderful forests with gushing waterfalls and clear blue lakes.

Near the famous Col du Mont-Cenis, the historic alpine pass crossed by Charlemagne, is the small town of **Lanslevillard** (preceding pages), surrounded by mountains shrouded in clouds, and containing some wonderfully fresh-looking paintings in its 15th-century chapel. Lanslevillard, like other nearby towns, was severely damaged during World War 2.

South of Grenoble, the landscape is wild and dangerous, with steep roads and peaks exceeding 2,000 metres (6,550 feet). This is the Vercors, a French resistance centre during World War 2 and a practice ground for the 1968 Olympics. **Pont-en-Royans** (preceding pages, inset) is built alongside a deep narrow gorge and surrounded by extraordinary scenery. The nearby town of Vizille is where in 1788 aristocrats and commoners decided to join forces and oppose the king. It was this meeting that led to the Revolution the following year.

The Hérault area of **Languedoc-Roussillon** (left) is known for its vineyards which become a glorious gold and red in the autumn. Located in the west of Mediterranean France, the region is one of the biggest vineyards in the world, with nearly all its population engaged in the business of growing grapes.

Small family-held patches are all over the hills and valleys, spreading around walled villages with Roman-tiled roofs. Women and men cover the vineyards with manure, often in the form of pressed grape skins, after the vintage. By winter, the new wine can be tasted and the year-round cycle of pruning and weeding starts all over again.

This region specializes in *vin ordinaire*, basic cheap wine. A flood of winegrowers poured into the area in the late 19th century, driven out of the hills by phylloxera, the disease that attacks vines. They tended to plant haphazardly instead of working out exactly where the right vine should be positioned to yield a quality product.

It is estimated that France has more than 1.2 million hectares (3 million acres) of vineyards, a huge area in proportion to the size of the country. The almost unrivalled reputation of France's wine is partly due to the soil, partly to the grapes, and partly to centuries-old expertise. A central institute of wine labelling oversees the definition and classification of France's vineyards, work which has been going on for almost 200 years. Field workers supervise activities at the local level and report back to the central body.

All the famous regions like Bordeaux, Burgundy and the Loire, have the *appellation contrôlée* guarantee of origin and standard, which means that the wine is derived from grapes grown only in that region and not a mixture from elsewhere. Lesser local wines earn the rank of 'VDQS', *Vin Délimité de Qualité Supérieure*. The date on a bottle of wine is also an indication of its taste and quality, because, with changing weather conditions, some vintages are better than others.

Peaches grow in the Loire Valley, lavender in the fields of Provence, apples in Normandy, truffles in the Périgord. But cactus and prickly plants sprout in the stony gardens of Èze (above right), a tiny village on the Côte-d'Azur.

This 'jardin exotique' is situated on a windy remote

mountain top above the blue Mediterranean. The view, a vast expanse of sky, horizon, water and craggy mainland, is positively breathtaking. Clouds sometimes cover the sun, making strange light patterns on this fascinating collection of flora and fauna.

Not many people live in Èze, which seems carved out of the tip of the cliff. This is a village for pedestrians only, and houses often open on to the roof level of those one street below.

Èze's desolate feeling is marred by a burgeoning tourist trade. Nevertheless it is still possible to imagine what life was like when this was a retreat in the 8th century and after, when Saracens swooped down on the area, looking for slaves.

'Paradise on earth' was how King Leopold of Belgium described the Côte-d'Azur, the magnificent coast that stretches from Marseille past **St Tropez** (following pages, inset) to Monaco. Here by the Mediterranean the air is softer, the sun brighter and the colours more vivid than anywhere else in France.

St Tropez used to be a quiet little fishing village visited by Parisians and the occasional artist or writer. But that was some time ago. Each summer this village of about 6,000 inhabitants swells to about 35,000, as holidaymakers pour in from all corners of the earth. Motorcycles buzz down the narrow cobbled streets and fabulous yachts nudge each other in the lovely port. Countless thousands of motorists inch along the tiny road into St Tropez, with traffic jams stretching for 5 or 6 km (3 or 4 miles).

The cafés provide the best ringside seat in all France to see the latest vogue in clothes. Each year there is another special 'look', a way of dressing that indicates the wearer is right up to date. This may be cowboy boots with embroidery on one side only, a braided hairdo with red-dyed fringe or a see-through cheesecloth shirt.

The topless fad began on the beaches of St Tropez, crowded sandy spots a short distance from the town. The show is still quite extravagant, with matrons and young beauties showing off their bodies under the baking sun.

Along the Riviera, as the Côte-d'Azur is also called, is one of the most celebrated wooded peninsulas in the world. A refuge for the rich and famous, **St Jean-Cap-Ferrat** (below) contains many superb villas and beautiful gardens, and is one of the most desirable residential areas in France. Near the tip of the peninsula is the Villa Mauresque which belonged to writer William Somerset Maugham, and a large building in the centre, Villa des Cèdres with its huge botanical garden, was owned by King Leopold II of Belgium. The Villa Ephrussi Rothschild, in another magnificent garden, was designed as a museum, and houses a miscellaneous collection of works which once belonged to a member of the Rothschild family. On display are oriental screens and carpets, porcelain, furniture, Impressionist paintings and Louis XVI costumes.

Beaulieu, the town on the mainland behind Cap-Ferrat, once claimed to have had only four days of frost in a period of 15 years. True or not, its sheltered situation has attracted many warm-weather seekers; in the 19th century, the British Prime Minister, the Marquess of Salisbury, designed and built a villa here.

The coastline between Beaulieu, which is close to Monaco, and **St Tropez** (left) on the way to Toulon, is legendary. There is Nice, city of expensive and luxurious

hotels, and venue of the fabulous Mardi Gras carnival on Shrove Tuesday. Cannes, a few miles down the coast from Juan-les-Pins where the Mistral wind seems to blow its hardest, was the watering hole of many 19th-century aristocrats including Queen Victoria. It comes alive during the film festival held in late spring when the famous Promenade des Anglais becomes the haunt of movie makers and film stars.

The beach at **Cannes** (above) is also a major attraction of the town. Beaches in France are never more crowded than in the month of August, the traditional French holiday period. At this time of the year, families pile into cars and flee the cities for the seaside or mountains. This massive exodus leaves behind empty towns, with shops and restaurants closed for an entire month, and fills resort areas to brimming capacity.

Attempts to reduce this mass migration by staggering holiday times have so far not been successful. Many families are devoted to a specific beach or rented villa to which they return every year at the same time and which they regard as an extension of their own home.

The lovely Mediterranean island of Corsica, part of France since 1769, is full of hidden villages and towns on crags or in green valleys. **Corte** (right), the old capital with about 5,500 inhabitants, is one of these.

Situated deep in the centre of the island, and protected by rivers on three sides, Corte is far away from the crowds of visitors who come each year to bathe along the island's

1,000 km (620 mile) coastline or climb its steep mountains.

In Ajaccio, capital of the island, the birthplace of Napoleon, there are plenty of reminders of the Emperor, with museums and statues dedicated to his memory. In Bastia, on the northern tip of Corsica, the busy commercial port dominates the town, while in Bonifacio, an ancient fortress town on a limestone cliff in the south, the tourist trade is all important.

But Corte is a living reminder of the short period from 1729 to 1769 when Corsica was an independent nation. General Jean-Pierre Gaffori, a native of Corte and Corsica's first leader, is honoured with a bronze statue in a square named after him. Pascal Paoli, who created a government and constitution for Corsica, is remembered in the same way. There are old houses, tiny streets and ancient fountains. The National Palace, once the residence of the Genoese controlling the island and then the parliament of independent Corsica, is now being restored.

Fortunately, hidden Corte is not completely immune from the famous fragrance of Corsica. This is a combination of wild flowers and scented herbs, a perfume which emanates from the island's thick undergrowth, the *maquis*. It is an overwhelmingly beautiful scent.

The people of Corte can be proud of their island, the third largest in the Mediterranean. It is a paradise of mountains and blue sea, of valleys and giant ferns, of beaches with silky sands and tiny coves beneath towering cliffs. It is peaceful and dramatic, quiet and wild.

Index

Acknowledgements

The publishers wish to thank the following organizations and individuals for their kind permission to reproduce the photographs in this book.

William Allard/Image Bank 45; Alain Choisnet/Image Bank 12–13, 17 inset, 18, 19, 22–23, 25; *Daily Telegraph* Colour Library 40 right; Dupin/Image Bank 34 below; C. & J. Fichter/Image Bank 52–53; Peter Frey/Image Bank 4–5, 14 above; Lawrence Fried/Image Bank 44; Francisco Hidalgo/Image Bank 2–3; Jessueld/Image Bank 42–43; Liard/Image Bank 16–17; Bullaty Lomeo/Image Bank 34–35 above, 49; Jean-Claude Lozuet/Image Bank 50–51, 60–61; Pascaud/Image Bank 56 inset; Provident/Image Bank 56–57; Rex Features/Sipa 12 left; Peter Roberts 28–29, 55; Paul Slaughter/Image Bank 33; Spectrum Colour Library 54, 60 inset, 62, 63; John Lewis Stage/Image Bank 1, 6, 39; Topham/Fotogram 8–9, 10, 11, 14–15, 20–21, 24, 26, 27, 30–31, 32, 35 below, 36–37, 38, 40 left, 41, 43 above right & below, 46–47, 48, 52 below, 53 below, 58, 59.

PDO 80-544